MW00426138

Astara ~ A Place of Light

www.astara.org

ISBN 9781547103942

Illustrations by Teodors A. Liliensteins

Published by Astara

FOREWORD

Most every truly mystical experience contains a mixture of normal level reality and supralevel reality. Each "happening" is next to impossible to describe because it is enacted mainly on another level or plane of life which defies description in physical plane words. Earlyne, in *Secrets of Mount Shasta,* comes as close as possible to describing such an experience, a happening which she and I shared. She was a great writer. She was always the writer and I have been the speaker.

In writing of our joint spiritual adventure she has combined the individual astral projections we both experienced, the psychic perceptions and inundations, and the physical plane events that enveloped us on all levels. She wove them into a tapestry of words as she narrated the story of our visit to one of the sacred places of the world.

As this journey occurred nearly half a century ago, I cannot in my memory (I am 85 as I write this) precisely differentiate between each of Earlyne's experiences and each of mine, and I really don't believe it matters. There were two basic ideas of the book which I am sure were uppermost in Earlyne's mind as she wrote it. One was to present and explain the remarkable spiritual properties in the atmosphere, in the meadows, trees, springs, streams, stones and caves of Mount Shasta. The second was to illustrate the kind of spiritual initiatory event many have experienced on Mount Shasta and at other spiritual sites around the world. Such experiences can and do occur in each of our lives.

Earlyne and I visited Mount Shasta in 1952. The day before we actually ascended the slopes, we obtained directions to the Mount and a fire permit from the Ranger's office in the town of Shasta. We had thought to do some outdoor cooking while on the Mount, but as the events of the journey unfolded, food never entered our minds.

Mount Shasta is indeed a hallowed place; has been so for we know not how many centuries. Modern visitors, in their continuing reverence, contribute additional eloquence to the "silent" voices that speak the Ancient Wisdom from its heights.

I returned to Mount Shasta but once. In August of 1986 I led a group of people on a California Spiritual Centers tour, which included a visit to the Mount. There were fifty of us who participated in a meditation about half way up the height. Occasional strangers passing by stopped to listen to us, some to join us, in our time of attunement.

First we asked to come in touch with the spirits of the American Indians for whom the Mount was a sacred place. We thanked them for their perspective of, and contributions to, the spiritual vibrations experienced there. We asked them to be present with us in our meditations as we addressed the four points of the compass in our version of the Indian way of prayer. Then we spent time silently inbreathing the elements of water, earth, fire, air and spirit of that radiant site.

We then asked to be overshadowed by the many Master Teachers for whom the Mount has historically served as either an occasional or a continuing abode. We requested that each of us be appropriately enfolded by the spiritual energies of their domain — that their lives become integral to our lives, and we asked the boon of taking with us, in definite if not immediately realizable form, the feeling of oneness with them which nearly every one of us felt at that time.

Then we separated — individuals or in groups of two or three — to find secluded niches for personal meditation. Half an hour later we reassembled for our return journey down the mountain.

I suggest that anyone, or any group, visiting the Mount follow a similar procedure. Simply to ascend the mountain and return isn't conducive to appreciating or experiencing the potent psychic, spiritual or mystical possibilities inherent in such a holy place. It isn't necessary to follow exactly the procedure I've described. Follow your own intuition. It is important to remember that spiritual expectations are usually best fulfilled in a spiritual atmosphere which combines the power of place with a receptive consciousness.

I hope Earlyne's telling of our experience inspires you on your spiritual Path. Remember that not encountering a similar episode is no indicator of any spiritual shortcoming in your life. These events may be dramatic, but they are not the goal. This experience sets us neither apart nor above anyone else. I'm sure the world is filled with persons of greater spiritual stature than either Earlyne or myself. The important matter is that you seek spirituality for its own sake, for its meaning in your life. We are all on the Path — each in his or her own way.

I hope that sharing our experience on Mount Shasta so many years ago helps you move further along your own Path in the present and future. I know Earlyne joins me in this wish for you.

Robert Chaney

Upland, California
October, 1998

INTRODUCTION

BACK IN 1952, my husband and I experienced a unique happening at Mt. Shasta in northern California. The unseen teachers who requested our presence there called it an "initiation by fire."

It was so singular a happening, I wrote a report about it when we returned to our home in Southern California. The teachers suggested we publish the report as a book. I felt the experience was too personal, too sacred — and should be locked secretly away in the archives of our hearts. The teachers suggested its message had an outreach and a need at that moment in the changing times of the approaching Aquarian Age. They felt the experience and the writing should be shared with seekers in the world of the esoteric, hoping it would offer guidelines to many whose lives it might touch and influence.

So we released the report as a book. It received widespread notice in the world of metaphysics, being highly acclaimed by most, but misunderstood by others.

Some journeyed to Shasta attempting to seek their own initiation there, even though they had been warned against such an effort. So disappointed were they, and so controversial were some opinions, we sought advice from the teachers who sent us there. Because I was distressed by adverse criticism — and still felt the experience too sacred to share — the teachers suggested the book be withdrawn from the public until a later time — a time when readers and seekers would more readily understand and receive the prophecies and the happenings the book offered.

Not until 1980 did we receive the signal from the spiritual Hierarchy to reissue the message. I was still apprehensive about sharing it, but was assured that "the world has turned many times since 1952" and that many now had need of such a sharing.

I think they felt I had spiritually matured enough so that incredulity on the part of some readers would no longer determine our course of action. They felt that those whom the book would benefit would far outnumber those whose minds could not comprehend the profound significance of the teachers, the message, and the prophecies.

So the beautiful book goes forth again — not to the glory of the two to whom it happened. Rather, to give to the world a new understanding of the approaching days of a new century — a century which will see the birth of a new Earth, a New Age and a New Human Being.

There are many whose lives this book will touch. It is my hope the touch will bring the baptism of Holy Spirit, a downpouring blessing from a realm now better understood. Some lives may be transformed. For those who find it incredulous, may I suggest the book be hid away until a year hence — then read again. Many changes are wrought with the turning tides of time. Perhaps the light of understanding will find its place in the unfolding awareness.

The Infinite Being works in myriad ways. In these quickening times, this outreach expands. The Divine Spirit seeks every possible way to make the message known. This published report is only one small "sending." But it has its place to fill as the assemblage of divinity and angels draw near Earth and its human lifewave, preparing us for our birth, our transition into the ethers of Aquarius.

Earlyne
June 9, 1981

SECRETS FROM MOUNT SHASTA

WELL DO I REMEMBER the night at our temple of Astara when, during one of our classes in mysticism, the Master Teacher Rama partially materialized. Accustomed as I am to beholding images of the Masters — in visionary form during meditation or as sudden flashes of spontaneous presences — his appearance should not have startled me. Nevertheless, the height of his misty form, the majestic brilliance of the light that wavered around him, and the flaming jewel that flashed in the headdress he wore were quite unusual manifestations.

Startling also was the fact that as he spoke to us his nebulous form slowly levitated, and was held suspended in midair near the ceiling of the room. But what astonished me even more was that, while his form was poised there in our midst, he called my name and asked that I step to his side. The church auditorium was filled to capacity, and all heard the words that he spoke — words which both delighted and bewildered me.

He asked that my husband, Robert, and I plan a trip to Mount Shasta during the months ahead. He informed me that another initiation was planned for us whenever we could make the journey. It delighted me because we had long been promised that another initiation was imminent, and that it would occur in unusual surroundings. We had never been given any indication just how or where it would happen. Also, we had long heard of Mount Shasta and the place it occupied in mystical lore.

It bewildered me, however, because at the time Rama imparted the message to me it was our intention that Robert would journey to Indiana and conduct seminars and classes at a spiritual retreat there, as he had done for many summers in the past, and we simply did not see how a trip to Shasta could be arranged to fit our planned schedule.

However, shortly thereafter our plans changed abruptly. Robert suddenly decided to resign from the teaching staff at the retreat center to devote more time to the expanding program of Astara. This must have been known already by the unseen Masters, for this change made possible the trip to Shasta.

Before we departed, we were given instructions from the Masters. We were told to take along camping equipment and our binoculars; to wear shoes with rubber soles for climbing. A camera was suggested to photograph any unusual manifestation that might occur. We were told to arrive at Shasta on a Sunday morning early, and to fast two days previously. We were to give no thought as to how to proceed once we arrived at Shasta, for we were assured of guidance.

We were both, however, shown a vision of some mammoth rocks and a cave, and we were told that this was what we were to search for. We were instructed to leave our car at a certain location and journey onward on foot; that we should not attempt to climb toward the snow-capped peaks of the Mount itself, but toward the top of one of the smaller peaks without snow.

Robert and I arrive at the city of Mt. Shasta, which nestles at the foot of the majestic mountain of Shasta. The mountain is named after a California tribe of Indians called the Shastas.

And so it was that we arrived in the city of Mt. Shasta on the Sunday morning of August 10, 1952, Robert in his blue denims and I in my slacks. It was very early and people were not in evidence. The sun had not yet completely broken through the dawn. We were quite hungry, having fasted since the Friday before, but since the command to fast had come from the Master, we gave no great thought to food, and started immediately for the road leading up Mt. Shasta itself.

About fifteen miles up the side of the Mount there is a government camp called *Panther Meadows.* The journey to this height was not at all pleasant. The dust was thick, and even though we drove with the windows of the car closed, still the dust poured in, choking us, and covering us and everything else in the car. The heat wave that had rocked the nation had also enveloped the town of Mt. Shasta. At this early hour the air was still chilly, however, and the further we drove up the mountainside the more pleasant the journey became.

It was a unique situation. We knew that within a short time the miles behind us would lie sweltering in the heat, yet ahead of us rose majestic Mt. Shasta with an enormous blanket of snow which seemed almost close enough for us to touch. As we neared Panther Meadows, the world beneath us faded into forgetfulness as our eyes beheld the vast expanse of nature's beautiful handiwork all about us.

Robert stands at the marker identifying a verdant green campsite known as Panther Meadows. *The meadow is the topmost point up the mountain beyond which most travelers cannot ascend. There are no roads proceeding upward—only a vast wilderness of trees and boulders.*

It is difficult to paint a word picture. There were the giant pines surrounding us on every side, towering in sky-piercing peaks of green. The sky, on this particular dawn, was an immense splash of vivid colors, as though Mother/Father God had taken a divine paintbrush and made great sweeps across this universe. In the east, where the sun was preparing to burst upon us, there were streaks of crimson and gold. In mid-heaven, wide patches of deep blue hung like a blanket over us, while in the west, where night clung to the horizon, the colors deepened into purple.

Below us and all about us were deep chasms, still held in the embrace of night. Sprinkled over the chasms were misty films of morning fog. They floated like scattered giant spider webs over the valleys below us, some dim and dark, like grieving ghosts over their beloved gardenspot. Others suspended like wondrous threads of silver, reminding me of a vision I once saw of a divine deva combing her silver hair outward to fly in the wind of her world.

Above and over all, Mt. Shasta rose like a Lord overshadowing his kingdom. In the approaching sunrise its peak poised like a magnificent white pearl, catching now a gleam, now a fleeting shadow, of the evaporating dawn.

We arrived at deserted Panther Meadows, chose our campsite and, gathering our wraps around us, sat for a quiet time just viewing the glories about us. We were 9000 feet up the side of the Mount. Then we followed arrows pointing the way to water, and found a mountain spring of the coldest, clearest water I have ever seen. It flowed right out of the ground, eddying into a little waterfall and stream, winding through the center of a large green meadow near our campsite.

I dip into the cold waters of the mountain stream which wends it way across the meadow. The waters rise from deep inside the earth as an on-flowing spring.

As we prepared for our long climb up the mountain, we were aware of an undercurrent of excitement which we could not seem to dispel, nor did we try. We knew we were on the threshold of an incomparable Adventure, and we faced it with anticipation. We had heard much about this mysterious Mount — tales about some mystical folk who dwelt there, remnants of lost Lemuria. Some were said to appear in the surrounding communities on rare occasions wearing long hair and flowing white garments. We had heard tales of vast fortunes hid away 'mid rocks and crags. We had heard of Temples soaring among the snows of the wondrous peak, from which flashed occasional strange lights. We had heard of enigmatic strangers who could make vicious animals lie down before them in meek submission.

We wondered what lay ahead of us. Would we meet the mysterious tribe of Lemurians? — Or come upon the shining Temple of the Sun? — Or find lost treasures of gems or gold? Would the Lemurians be the hierophants for a ceremony of initiation in the halls of the majestic temple of the flashing lights? We had a great faith in our hearts that, if we but obeyed the orders given us, we would come down from Shasta different than when we journeyed upward. And we did.

YOU MUST BE AWARE that I cannot tell all the details of our experience on this singular journey, but I shall tell all that I may without betraying secrets which I am sworn to keep. To those who have not themselves been aware of some similar sort of spiritual, psychic or mystical experience, that which I am about to relate will seem utterly unbelievable, and I am sure some might find it even amusing. To those who have had, or to those who have even read of, such experiences, these related

happenings will only help them better to realize that mortals can be lifted up into immortal realms and return again to be mortal and normal.

And so it was that we prepared ourselves for our journey up the Mount. As we returned to our campsite after our visit to the stream, we were both aware that by our side walked an unseen one who would show us the way. His presence was unmistakable. We did not question the identity for we could sense that the guide was one to trust. We took with us our thermos filled with cold water from the spring, our camera, and our binoculars. We both wore warm jackets, though we knew that some of the journey would be in great heat.

Even though our guide was not visible to us, we intuitively learned some facts about him. We knew he carried with him some sort of guide-stick — much like an elongated flashlight, although the lights he flashed to guide us were lights the ordinary vision could not have seen. When we were uncertain, one of us always caught the flash of the light ahead of us and followed. It reminded me of a beloved old hymn, a favorite of mine, called *Follow the Gleam.*

The climbing was not easy. In fact it was dreadful. Such a foot journey would easily discourage any who could not discern the glory which lay at the end of it. The heart would have to be filled with a burning eagerness and desire to attain the goal at the end of the journey, or the climb toward it would be so completely discouraging as to make the trip unthinkable. Only a "pot of gold" at the top could have ever induced me to make that climb. I now carry that "gold" within my heart and there isn't enough material gold in the universe to induce me to part with it. Were I approached today by one who offered a fortune in earthly wealth to recant and deny the words of this story, I would not. I could not, for they are a record of truth, and I would not deny them for the proverbial "thirty pieces of silver."

It did not take long for us to realize that the climb itself was another test on the Path toward God-realization. We knew that there were those watching to ascertain whether or not we had the courage to face the hardships of the climb in order to attain the goal ahead ... which was to be one of the supreme spiritual experiences of our lives. No offer was made to help us, save the flash of the light which guided our way.

All must be tested before initiation. Sometimes the tests come in daily living, and the initiation itself is only a glorious ceremony culminating the past efforts. In these particular initiations one does not, at the time of the ceremony, need to endure dangers and hardships, for past months and years prove the record of the disciple.

Other initiations require thorough and rigorous tests to be encountered at the time of the ceremony, in addition to tests met, withstood and overcome in daily living. Our initiation at Shasta was to be a combination of both. We had faced and apparently surmounted the tests of our daily lives, or we would not have been invited to another initiation. The climb we were now engaged upon marked the climactic test before the ceremony itself. The climb, however, was the only hardship for us, and we were not faced with other travails during the entire initiation.

The sun, rising now into the heavens, already rayed heat upon us. There were long expanses upward where there were no trees ... nothing but mammoth boulders. Robert removed his jacket and tied it about his waist. I did not follow his example, for my arms break out with heat rash when exposed to the direct rays of the sun, and already I suffered from exposure during the days of our drive north. The boulders themselves presented an almost impossible blockade. Robert is unusually agile for a man who does little physical training, and has exceptional endurance. The only point in my favor is that I am slim. I am neither agile nor enduring, nor do I take gracefully to primitive life.

So there we were, struggling up the side of the mountain. Sometimes it all seemed silly. If we had built our hopes upon surmise instead of a definite KNOWING that the Masters expected us, we would surely have turned back and declared the whole thing ridiculous. There was Robert, wearing blue denims and a sweater, with his warm jacket tied about his waist, hot, very dirty and dusty, with his camera dangling from one hand and the thermos from the other. There was I, wearing slacks and my warm jacket, arms broken out with heat, tired, hot and dusty, carrying binoculars suspended in their case about my neck ... and complaining bitterly.

Why, I reasoned, could not the Masters have brought the experience of initiation to us at home? Why did we have to climb all over this rocky mountain? And besides, why couldn't we eat for days? Did they want us to starve? And what if a big snake suddenly popped up its head just when I was clutching a big boulder, trying to gain my footing? And how could we be sure one of those boulders wouldn't loosen and come crashing down upon us? So what if they *had* been there for thousands of years ... still .... And, I wonder if that guide knew what he was doing, because if so, why did he have to bring us up the side of the very most rugged peak instead of one of those others with shade trees on it? And besides, my back ached and my feet hurt, and I doubted if I could ever get my fingernails to look decent again because they were all broken and dirty and stained ... and besides ....

Ah, well, I guess it's my prerogative to jokingly and even joyfully complain ... especially since I meant not one word I uttered, and I knew I could voice my complaints aware all the while that nothing, *absolutely nothing,* could actually make me change my mind about my goal. I reserved the right to complain, even though I knew the answer to all my "whys." I knew why we had to climb that awful mountainside, and in my heart I did it cheerfully, and even approved the Masters' making it difficult to attain ... but I still reserved the right to utter my discomfort laughingly and loudly.

We sat down often to get our breath and rest. When we did so, we always scanned the mountainside with binoculars, and also the surrounding scenery. We had been climbing for about two hours when, during one of these "looks," Robert suddenly rose from where he was sitting, never ceasing to gaze through the glasses, and stood poised there, staring upward, with the binoculars focused on something which he seemed to be straining to see better.

"Do you see something?" I asked.

He did not answer for a long time, but kept his gaze focused upon a certain spot. Then he lowered the binoculars and handed them toward me. He did not say yes or no. He had a strange look on his face. He simply said, "Take a look."

I raised the glasses toward the spot which had claimed his attention. There, caught in the view of the glasses, was the exact scene shown to us in the vision we had seen. It was unmistakable.

"That's it! That's the spot!" I exclaimed. I would have hurriedly put away the glasses, preparing to rush toward it, but Robert stayed me.

"Look again," he said, "and look carefully." I raised the glasses again and held them steadily fixed upon the spot. Then I understood what had caused Robert to rise to his feet and stand gazing at it for so long without answering my queries.

I saw the small light flash again which we had seen while climbing, and which had guided us. But this time the light grew until it became a large ball of white light. Then it exploded with a blinding flash over a certain rock. From the explosion there poured forth something vaguely resembling smoke, filled with flashes of lightning. The center of the light boiled like the molten sea. The smoke quickly seemed to solidify ... if you can imagine solidified smoke ... and rapidly formed into a glorious, blazing star of light.

This brilliant star hung there over the rock, with the heart of it sending forth rays, as if the sun had caught the light of a giant flashing diamond. Then, suddenly, it was as if an unseen hand reached out and touched one of the star points and gave the whole star a twirl, causing it to look like a blazing torch in the hands of someone twirling it rapidly in front of them. And then, it completely vanished.

I am sure the whole vision lasted not more than a moment. I lowered the glasses. I looked at Robert, and he looked at me. We did not speak. But our thoughts went back together to the story of another Star. We remembered suddenly the Three Wise Men from the East who had set out on a journey. They, too, had followed a light, and had seen a Star shining over a certain stable in days of long ago. They had called theirs the Star of Bethlehem. Was this another such Star, or had we just seen the Star of Astara, which is the Star of a New and Coming Age?

THE SILENCE between us continued. We did not want to speak, for the moment seemed sacred. The day suddenly did not seem too warm. Robert removed his camera from its case. He turned it toward the rocks over which the star had shone and snapped a picture.

Then, as he moved closer to the rocks, I heard him ask our unseen guide to reproduce the light of the star on film so that we might share with others some of the wonders of our experiences ... and he took another picture.

(When the pictures were returned from the developing laboratory we were profoundly grateful to discover a light over the rocks which our camera caught on the film. The pictures are reproduced on the next page for you.)

This is the
first picture
Robert snapped...

...this is the
second picture,
showing the light

We started onward toward the Rock without speaking, and had gone only a few steps when a voice called to us ... a human voice ... the voice of a man. Not having fully recovered from the effects of our vision, the sound of a voice not only startled but shocked us, for we had thought ourselves utterly alone on the side of the Mount. But there, not far from us, sitting on a rock, was a man.

I wish so much that I could say he was like a man from another world. I wish I could say he had long tresses and wore a flowing white robe and sandals — that he resembled the mysterious lost Lemurians, the gods of antiquity, waiting to touch us with his wand of power and transform us instantly into radiant initiates. But I cannot.

He was not unlike any other man one would meet on the street of any city. He had black hair and combed it straight back from his forehead. He wore a short-sleeved shirt, high at the throat. He wore white slacks and, ah, yes ... there *was* something different! The belt he wore. It seemed to be made of old silver or pewter, interwoven with strands of leather. It was fairly wide, and carved on it were the signs of the zodiac.

His arms were very brown, and about each wrist he wore wide, tight bracelets of the same substance as his belt, except that in the center of the pewter, prominently displayed on each bracelet, was the All-Seeing Eye. Later, on close examination, we discovered that this Eye was made of some mysterious gem which had no color of its own, yet seemed to reflect the color of all the things surrounding it, as a mirror or a clear crystal might. On his feet he wore rubber-soled sandals.

I was disappointed. Well, I thought, here is our "mysterious stranger," but why couldn't he look "different?" My disappointment lasted only a fleeting moment, for, as we approached him, I saw his eyes. Large brown eyes they were, and sad. Sometimes the shadows in them made them appear even black. Between his eyes, I noticed the telltale indentation which becomes apparent in the forehead of one who spends much time in deep meditation.

But just now his eyes twinkled as he greeted us. "Hail!" he called to us, smiling. I presume we appeared fairly stupid, for we had been staring at him, speechless, and had climbed toward him, too startled to speak. We answered his hail. I wanted to begin a long series of questions. I wanted to know how he got there, and why we had not even seen him before, and where he came from. But somehow the questions seemed childish. I reasoned that he would tell us these things if he wished us to know them.

Robert reached him first and held out his hand. "I'm Robert Chaney," he said. "I know," the man replied, "I've been waiting. I am Idosa." He extended his hand to meet Robert's and it was then that I knew peace of mind. He doesn't resemble the ancient Lemurians, I thought, but could he possibly be a spaceman from a distant star? — A representative of the universal Order of Melchizedek, the Order of initiates which we knew to be existent not only on Earth but throughout various planetary systems?

"Follow me and we shall find a cooler place to chat," he said, as he led us upward and toward a tiny oasis of trees where apparently there was water, for all was green around the trees. This retreat lay somewhat out of our path toward the Rock, and we probably would not have sought it, but did not hesitate to follow him there. It was as we thought; there was water. There was another mountain spring, and the Stranger asked if we would not like to wash away some of the dust and perhaps immerse our tired feet in the stream.

We might have wondered why he, too, did not wish to do the same, but observation disclosed that he was neither dusty nor, apparently, tired. He asked if he might borrow the use of our thermos, then excused himself while we shed some of our dusty garments and rinsed the dust from our bodies. We plunged our feet in the stream — but not for long. For even though they had been very hot, the mountain water was far too cold for a leisurely dip.

In a little while we joined him. He sat, cross-legged, on a patch of grass. We sat down with him.

"In the vast ranges of the Andes in South America," he said, "there grows a peculiar herb, the tea of which can banish your weariness, and also better prepare you for your experiences up there." He nodded toward the mountain top, and slightly lifted his eyes in the direction of the Rock. "I have taken the liberty of making the tea in your thermos," he explained as he poured the cap of the thermos full. "Shall we share a cup?"

He took the first sip, and passed it to me. I did not hesitate, but followed suit. The tea tasted of something vaguely familiar but I never could place it. It was not good, not bad ... but by the

time we had each finished a cup, over which we lingered for some time, the effect of the herb was obvious. I do not mean that we experienced any change in our consciousness, such as one would if imbibing intoxicants. I mean that our bodies were gradually being renewed. The weariness, the hunger were slowly vanishing. I faced the remainder of the climb with eager anticipation rather than reluctance.

"We have called the upcoming ceremony your initiation by fire. It is not the ultimate Fire Initiation — you could not yet endure it. But it *is* a baptism in a fiery substance of higher voltage dedicated to opening your awareness toward a deeper understanding of the Drama of the Heavens.

"It is this cosmic Drama which is symbolized in carvings on temples, obelisks, tombs, pyramids, triumphal arches and statuary all over the planet — marking the presence of the Great Ones who came long ago from the starry depths of the solar heavens to leave their mark on this holy but unhappy planet you call Earth — but which *we* call *Tara*. (We thought of the name of our church and Mystery School which we had named *Astara*. We had been told by our unseen Masters to call it by this name and it was explained that Astara meant "a place of Light." We wondered if Astara could possibly be linked significantly to Tara, the name of our Earth once it was purified and had passed through its own solar initiation.)

IDOSA CONTINUED: "You already know that myths, legends, parables, riddles, superstitions and symbols all contain a limited hidden knowledge of ancient truths and mysteries. These legendary 'tales' have been bequeathed to human beings so that a fragment of truth may always remain extant and available despite the fury, the superstitions, destruction and havoc wrought by utterly fanatic and unenlightened zealots throughout the ages.

"The temples, pyramids, arches and obelisks remain to speak of a cosmic Drama — based on truths written in the heavens. The starry skies reveal a drama of the ages. They tell the tale of humankind's sublime destiny. They reveal the eternal story of the Christos, the solar initiate; the mystery of the virgin birth; of the dying yet resurrected 'savior' — eternally symbolizing the drama of the human soul, its fall into matter, its struggle to overcome the trials and temptations of Earth, its final victory over the carnal nature through crucifixion, and its ultimate Ascension into a new cosmic birth and being — its release from the hold of matter and its final return to its true estate as a Child of God.

"You will come to know that all this is written in the skies, formed by the stars — a cosmic Drama which no creed of humanity can change, deface or erase. A Drama eternally transferred into allegories, parables and legends, later to pen and parchment rolls and scriptures — and brought to birth in Orders on Earth, such as primitive Masonry.

"The cosmic Drama embraces the movement of the stars in constellations which follow an established universal law from which there can be no deviation. An initiation, such as the one upon whose threshold you stand, can help reveal the Greater Mystery of *Arcane* or *Philosophic Initiation* — but ultimately, each initiate must accomplish the *Great Work* in and for oneself, in the depths of the starry space within each self.

"Each must come to realize that the goal of humankind is to achieve purification and perfection of the soul through purity and love in daily life in the substance of matter. This is the *Great Work* in action — to awaken and bring into manifestation the Christos asleep within through the crucifixion of the carnal nature upon the altar-cross of purification and unselfish service.

"This is the eternal search for the Holy Grail. It is the alchemical transmutation of lead into gold — the carving away of the dross to reveal the true Philosopher's Stone. It is unearthing the lost treasure, *the pearl of great price*. It is attuning once again to the mysterious *Lost Word*. It is — finally — finding the kingdom of God within each human soul.

"This search can never be fulfilled through creed and dogma — only through initiation. Only through such a personal 'ordeal' can the One God be truly known, the One Supreme Being, with the sun, the moon and the stars performing as minor divinities, or forces. And the gods, the goddesses, the archangels, the angels, the deities, the Masters, the Heroes, and, finally, the human initiates serving as lesser divinities in form.

"All this you will better understand when you return once again to your work in Astara of the earth plane. So think, pray and rest — and know that you are blest."

As we sipped the tea together, he talked. Sometimes he would cease for a period and gaze out across the wide expanse of beauty about us, as if he saw much more than we could see ... as indeed he could. We hoped he would explain to us how he came to be there. He did give us a vague explanation intermittently, as he explained other mysteries.

"When the space beings first came to inhabit Earth, there existed Atlantis, and it was there that the Mysteries rose to their highest pinnacle. Atlantis and its Mystery Schools were flourishing at their peak when Egypt was yet in its childhood and India was in the bloom of youth. From the heart of the great continent

flowed four principal rivers toward the four points of the Earth. Atlantis saw the return of the space gods to Earth. And Atlantis saw the destruction of a mighty civilization and the passing of Earth through a cosmic initiation.

"Now I would speak about the changing face of Earth at this Aquarian time. Because Earth, as a great planetary entity, is about to undergo another cosmic initiation, we cannot speak of the planet and its ongoing destiny without becoming involved in the Drama of the Heavens. Earth is a part of that cosmic Drama. To understand the current happenings, we must enlarge our scope to include the surrounding heaven and spiritual planes.

"In the days when the Mysteries prevailed — during the reign of the great Hierophants, the Ptahs and the Magi — the Drama of the Heavens was enacted and understood by those who entered into and passed the supreme initiation. In the dim past of humankind's beginning, the space gods brought to early human beings of Earth a link-up with the divine hierarchy. They established what has been called the Mysteries. Intermarrying with the daughters of Earth, they created the 'children of renown' — that is, children with an earth mother and a god father. These beings were far superior to the human beings of Earth of that time, and it was into their keeping that the space gods placed the destiny of the Mysteries.

"It was through them that the Hierarchy was established on Earth through the Mysteries. The Mysteries were taken into every country — first into South America, in Peru, Bolivia, Yucatan, Brazil, Mexico. Then Egypt, Greece, Cambodia, Tibet, China, India. Wherever the space people made a settlement, there was established also a School of the Mysteries. Its purpose was to disseminate knowledge to the people of Earth, propelling them forward and upward toward a greater understanding of themselves, their world and the Divine Being.

"The basic principles of the Mysteries to be instilled in humanity's consciousness were:

1 . The existence of God, the Supreme Being.

2.   Operating under and through Mother-Father God, the divine hierarchy, composed of the gods and goddesses.

3.   The immortality of the human soul.

4.   The journey of the human soul through the world of matter ultimately to establish the fulfillment of his or her own destiny as an evolved divine being, and

5.   Ultimately a Universal Family, not only among all beings of Earth, but as they were interrelated with other planetary beings in their solar system and in the universe.

"Candidates undergoing initiation had revealed unto them the secrets of the Drama of the Heavens. The cornerstone of knowledge was that the First Great Cause was Spirit. From the womb of Spirit poured forth myriad fragments called *souls*. And from the soul was projected a lesser fragment, a human personality. This individualized soul, or personality, dwelt first in the etheric realm. To evolve into godhood, it was required that each soul "fall into matter." Each must take upon him or herself a coat of skin. Each must become embodied in a form of matter. For this purpose was the earth plane formed.

"Since matter — or the earth plane — is the lowest manifestation of Spirit, it was recognized by the initiates as "hell," or the temporal place of progression. It was the plane of "outer darkness," being furthest from the light of Spirit. It was the "below" into which souls "fall" to gain wisdom and understanding by experiencing both happiness and sorrow, joy and suffering, ecstasy and pain.

"Thus the earth plane was not a hell plane in itself — it was a plane where the soul was exposed to both heaven and hell. Each was given free will through which to make individual choices and establish his or her own pace toward future god-hood. Initiation was presented for the purpose of revealing to each individual soul that they possessed their own inner potential to break the bonds and limitations of their form of matter and express, momentarily, their godhood. Returning once again to their "brain" consciousness, they were ever after aware of the higher planes and their own higher potential, and understood that the struggle toward that highest attainment lay within their grasp.

"Each initiate understood that the soul had originally existed in a pure undefiled state; that it fell from its original purity to assume a form in the realms of matter, the purpose being to experience successive states of consciousness — sufferings and joys, pain and pleasure, on its journey back to its original estate in the heart of Deity.

"The Mysteries were ultimately divided into two levels to accommodate humanity's progression. One was called the Lesser Mysteries and one the Greater Mysteries. To the Lesser Mysteries gravitated the ordinary soul, content to be given symbolic initiation — which revealed the knowledge that it was an immortal soul overshadowed by spiritual beings, and that it would live after death. It sought no further than this understanding.

"The Lesser Mysteries constituted ceremonial or ritualistic initiation which served to bind the masses together. The Greater Mysteries existed for the true seekers — those who sought their own individual spiritual development and illuminated consciousness. Many became priests, priestesses, and initiators. And many experienced an initiation by fire.

"In all the Mysteries God was symbolized as light. The most perfect outer representative of that light was the sun, representing divine fire. This solar fire had little in common with our vulgar, gross fire. Rather, it was an occult, mysterious, supernatural form of an unburning, unheated celestial fire. Such a fire represented the inner light which held within its heart the soul of all things, the wisdom of the ages. In the innermost heart of each person, it is known as the soul, buried in darkness, entombed in the physical form.

"The purpose of the Fire Initiation is to transmute the gross into divine light, causing each person to become fully conscious of the celestial or spiritual fire burning within. There are no human words that can bring about this awakening, this realization. It can only come into manifestation through an inner awakening and a growth into a new understanding. The intent and purpose of the Fire Initiation has never changed. It is to burst asunder the bonds of error and darkness which hold the soul bound to a prison house of matter.

"In the Mysteries, the inner fire was always called *the ineffable light,* the all-pervading element. It is this inmost divine fire which the Great Ones establish as a reality when the soul merges with it at the peak of the Fire Initiation. Once having split asunder the bondage of ignorance, its flames never again expire. It will hold the soul evermore aligned with, attuned to and harmonious with the light of the god-self, that true ineffable light which is God."

THEN HE SPOKE of ancient temples and pyramids in Peru, in Yucatan, in China, in Tibet, and in Egypt. We asked if there were temples of the Mysteries on top of Mt. Shasta.

We experienced some degree of disappointment to hear him say, "No ...," but then he added, "There are no more outer temples — that is, temples that can be seen by human eyes. However, for centuries, atop a certain mountain peak, is the one we call the *Greater Temple*. The Greater Temple houses a Hall of Initiation.

"Inside the heart of the mountain is the *Lesser Temple*. Inside the Lesser Temple is what you would call a Museum. Inside that Museum is an invaluable array of documents, scrolls and records which reach far back into ageless time. In the Lesser Temple is also a Council Hall. It is there that those of us of the Order come to sit in council with one another.

"You see, I frequently leave my home to dwell in the cities as you do — " I waited, hoping breathlessly he would reveal to which city or cities he referred, but he did not. "There comes a time — perhaps once or twice a year — when we find it needful to journey here to the Lesser Temple, and spend some time within. Sometimes some of the other Brothers or Sisters are here also, and sometimes I am alone. So it would be a mistake to say that we always dwell here on this Mount, for we do not. Nor am I called Idosa in the cities.

"Sometimes comes a message that one of the Great Ones plans to hold Council here, or in the Greater Temple. When that happens, I — and others who are so notified — come. There are initiates living in various centers all over the Earth, though they are few in number. The Council sometimes concerns itself with some current world problem — not that they plan to solve it necessarily, for these things are left primarily to be worked out by leaders in high places here on Earth. But the Master does present it to us and makes suggestions about the part we might play in connection with it.

"Sometimes it relates to a great new invention already brought into being by science. Sometimes it concerns one which now needs to be brought about. Sometimes it is simply to teach us more about nature's laws and how to use them in our lives. It all depends upon which of the Masters appears and with what particular school of thought he or she is engaged. If it is the Cosmic Overlord, it is always concerned with diffusing some measure of truth and understanding to aid humankind toward greater light and liberation

— the ultimate salvation. Often he will notify us that an initiate is about to present or participate in an important seminar some of us should attend — because a new aspect of truth of the new age is about to be released.

"And so — I have been here on this occasion about a week, attending to other work and waiting for you, for I knew you were on your way. You have seen the Greater Temple many times in your astral journeys, and also the Lesser Temple. You will not climb just now to the Greater Temple, for reaching it presents quite a complicated problem. But now let us journey to the Lesser Temple."

The sun rose higher in the heavens as he talked with us. He spoke of many things which had happened to us since our last initiation. He soothed our apprehensions regarding some of the decisions we had made which altered our lives and assured us they had been right decisions. He spoke to us of the heavy yoke of leading Astara, and the grave responsibilities connected with it.

He warned that even though the Masters watched over Astara and its teachings, we two would be called upon to make many decisions without the help of the Teachers, for it was the desire of the Order that we develop our own wisdom. Their major aim was for the proper teachings to issue from Astara, and the solving of most of our material problems would rest with us.

What a difference the remaining climb presented. Idosa hardly seemed to climb at all; it was more as if he "walked upward," if that phrase could describe the lightness with which he stepped from stone to stone. We also seemed to exert little effort. Whether it was the invigorating vibrations of this mysterious Mount, the effects of the herb tea, or the presence of the remarkable Stranger with us, it would be difficult to say. Nevertheless, the journey upward was completed in an amazingly short time with very little expenditure of energy on our part.

Idosa reached the great boulder first ... the one over which the star had flashed. He stood there above us, his figure silhouetted against the sky. It was then for the first time that I caught, clairvoyantly, the colors of his aura, and I knew that even though he dressed and spoke as any ordinary person from any ordinary city, here was a highly developed initiate, perhaps even an ascended Master.

And then he stretched his hands upward, and we knew he wanted to pray. He spoke in a low voice as he asked the blessings of "the Almighty and Everlasting Spirit" upon us. As he spoke, my mind flashed to remembrance of another who removed his sandals because he stood on holy ground, and I suddenly wanted to remove my shoes. I felt I was about to enter vibrations so sacred as to warrant the removal of the earthly dust from my feet. I more easily understood then why, in eastern lands, it is customary for worshippers to remove their shoes before entering a temple or a teacher's dwelling place, as a mark of their humility and reverence.

Then, we three stepped up to the Rock together. We stood looking down into what appeared to be a grotto or cave which never could have been seen by eyes further down the mountain. How cleverly the Cave was concealed. It would be a mistake to say that a rock or rocks covered the entrance, yet you would never know the Cave was there until you had almost walked into it. Around the entrance were many large boulders and though they did not cover the entrance they kept the eyes from discerning the Cave unless one deliberately searched for it.

Let me take a moment here to describe our surroundings. The boulder over which the star had flashed stood on the edge of what I have called a "grotto," but which probably would be better described simply as a deep, wide entrance surrounded by huge boulders. It was some of these boulders which partially covered the opening which we knew to be the Cave. However, to reach the entrance to the Cave one had to scramble down into the enormous hole, and over the great rocks.

Idosa went first. He stepped lightly across them, and then turned to give me a hand. It must have been extremely amusing to find me laboriously edging from rock to rock. It was no easy thing for me, I can tell you. I could not maintain my balance and frequently had to bend almost double to avoid slipping off a rock. Robert, like Idosa, stepped skillfully across them. Between the two of them, they managed finally to maneuver me over to the entrance of the Cave with no mishap. They had quite a laugh at me, and Robert still laughs. Nevertheless, I stoutly maintain that the going was treacherous. A foot caught between those rocks would not be funny, and a slip of the foot could cause the whole body to be subjected to a nasty fall. And besides, there was the possibility of that proverbial snake! But, of course, there was Idosa's hand in front of me, and Robert's behind me, so truly there was little to fear.

My real fear came a moment later. As we neared the Cave entrance we could see that it was as black as the blackest night. Instinctively, I hesitated. Idosa entered and turned to wait for me to follow after him. Suddenly I was seized with an incredible terror. Who was this Stranger, and how did we know we could trust him? After all, I reasoned, I had heard weird tales about people lost in caves and never found. I had an overwhelming impulse to turn and scramble out of the grotto and down the side of the mountain. I peered into the darkness ....

Laborious approach to the dark entrance of the Mystic Cave...

*Beyond the entrance,
the glories of Initiation?
Or only darkness?...*

JUST INSIDE THE ENTRANCE Idosa stood, waiting. His head was slightly lowered and his eyes closed, as if he would project mental strength to me. As I still hesitated, I suddenly remembered the initiations of the Master Jesus in the scripture, *The Aquarian Gospel.* I recalled how it was with him when he, too, had been confined in dark caverns and certain tempters had endeavored to plant fear in his mind and destroy his faith in the holy ones who had placed him there. I remembered what he said to them. He had rebuked them, commanding their departure. He had expressed anew his faith in the holy ones. By so doing, he passed another test.

Why this experience of the Master should be remembered at this particular time, I do not know. I only know that suddenly I was no longer afraid. I turned and looked at Robert. He nodded his head to me, encouraging me to proceed.

Perhaps you think I was foolish for doubting and yet I wonder how you may have reacted. You must have read also that initiation sometimes requires tremendous courage and bravery, and failing the test could possibly cost the life of a candidate. Of course, I never for a moment felt that we were entering into something which might cost either of our lives. I simply felt the human fear of the immense darkness stretching before us and the unknown territory of an unexplored and unlighted Cave. Robert also had a struggle — he spoke about it to me later. But after he nodded to me, I felt still more assurance, and stepped toward Idosa.

After entering the Cave, there were more rocks and boulders leading down and down into the shadows, but we could see where they ended and level ground began. I breathed a sigh of relief to reach that level ground, and was even more pleasantly surprised to discover that it was sand, and quite soft. Idosa suggested we rest a moment to get our breath and adjust our eyes to the darkness. As we sat, we became aware that the darkness was not so dark after all. Somewhere in the distance, back in the Cave, a faint nebulous light burned and its reflections reached us there on the sandy floor.

We began to observe our surroundings. Now I cannot tell you all the details, as I have said. But I will tell you what I can. It was as if the walls of the Cavern emitted some sort of mellow light. Perhaps some of the rocks were indeed minerals which glow in the dark ever so faintly ... so dimly that, standing on the outside of the Cave, in bright sunlight, the inside of the Cavern would appear totally black. The temperature of the Cave was quite cool compared to the burning heat outside, yet it was not cold. Idosa told us the temperature remained constant inside the Cave the year 'round, in spite of bitter cold weather there on the mountain during the winter months and the blazing heat of midsummer.

Idosa suggested we explore the walls of the Cave, and we did so eagerly. The beauty of it was wondrous to behold. It all appeared to be the handiwork of God, with nothing added by humans. Some of the rocks in the walls seemed to be emerald, for they emitted a soft green gleam in the pale light. I do not mean that they gave off a green light. I mean there were huge glowing solid green slabs of rock, both rough and polished, embedded in the walls, which in the dimness seemed to transcend the dullness of common green rock. Interspersed among the green there were slabs of rust red perforated with white streaks, reminding me of children's marbles. And then there would appear great formations of crystal-like stones; some of the granite with white streaks, and some of shiny slate which resembled glowing black in the shadows about us. The entire Cave appeared to be a completely natural one and I feel sure this was so.

Idosa let us explore for a while, and then he suggested we follow him further into the Cave. We had walked quite a distance when Idosa turned suddenly from the main route of the tunnel, and led us toward an unobtrusive upstanding slab. He stepped behind it. There, well hidden from view, was the entrance to another Cave. But one had to stoop to enter it. We followed him through the entrance and into an Inner Room. The accompanying picture is not of the Cave we were in, but is one of the several similar caves in the vicinity.

One of the caves found in the vicinity of Mt. Shasta. The walls of the Cave of the Mystic Circle resembled this one.

It indeed resembled a huge room. Apparently this one had been fashioned by the hand of humans, for it seemed to be organized with some well-laid plan in mind. For instance, the walls of this Cavern Room formed a complete circle. The walls were of the same various colors we had seen in the outer room. I do not mean that there were furnishings that human beings would need, but directly in the center of the circular cave was a low stone slab. It was only about a foot in height and formed in the shape of a triangle. At the point of the triangle sat a tiny receptacle which appeared to be a unique lamp, for there burned from it a small blue flame. I hesitate to affirm this, but apparently this was our only source of light. The dim light which had reached even into the distant outer room had apparently emanated from this infinitesimal blue flame. It seemed impossible, and still does, yet I never did behold any other source of light, unless the rocks themselves were fluorescent. Also, there was something else strange about the light. It emitted no heat, nor did it smoke. It just burned steadily without a flicker.

We sat down cross-legged on the sand of the floor, and Idosa opened the thermos again. We drank more of the tea together while Idosa spoke to us of the temple in which we sat. This, he said, was the Lesser Temple, and it was here he came when he wished to retreat from the world. He told us there was an obscure door which led out of this Cave — which he called the Cave of the Mystic Circle — and he said that behind that door would be found quite a comfortable place to bide awhile, although he did not ever take us into those quarters. I glanced around, hoping to discern the door. I never did locate it. It was either very well concealed or it was one of those mysterious portals which opened by a secret Word of Power or touch — like those in the pyramids and temples of Egypt.

The Cave of the Mystic Circle was wholly bare save for the triangular slab of stone and the blue light. So we had not actually seen, nor were we to see, anything at all unusual there, in material substance, on top of Mount Shasta. Any wanderer might explore the outer Cave — and even this inner Cave — and still not obtain any secrets. If by chance one discovered the inner Cave, the triangle of stone would arouse curiosity, but it would remain as silent as the Sphinx so far as revealing any mysteries.

Yet, bare as it was, it was filled to capacity with an invisible SOMETHING. The very air was so highly charged one could almost feel electricity flashing about, as if the room were saturated with the power of it. Idosa explained that it was in this room that many Councils were held, and an occasional Initiation. He said that not many of the candidates for initiation were brought to the Mystic Circle in person as we had been. Instead, they were brought in their astral bodies while their physical bodies slept, and most of them did not remember the Ceremony at all. He indicated that he did not attend all of the Councils — only those to which he was especially invited. He said that the Lesser Temple was frequently deserted, but that some member of the Order who knew of it might journey there at any time to withdraw from outer activity for awhile.

I want to digress for a moment, to urge you to dismiss any idea you might have about making this journey unless you are invited to a personal initiation. I do not refer to a trip to Mount Shasta itself — for such a pilgrimage is a wonderful thing — but never attempt to discover the Cave of the Mystic Circle. First, you could not, for one would need to be led to find it. Second, if you did find it you would encounter only the gloomy darkness. However, I would like to urge all who possibly can to some day plan a trip to Mt. Shasta to experience not only its beauty but the high spiritual vibrations.

ALL TRACE OF A TWINKLE left the eyes of Idosa as he talked to us. His voice was low and very gentle. He seemed to have entered into deep contemplation, and for that matter so had we. I felt not unlike the time I was baptized when I was nine. I remember I prayed

fervently then, as I walked into the water, and I became keenly aware that even now, as I sipped the tea, I was again praying zealously in my heart. I do not know what the herb was supposed to induce. I only know that, as we sipped it, all thoughts of fear, all thoughts of the outside world, seemed to slip away as we relaxed completely under its influence and the persuasion of the low voice speaking to us. I know that as my body relaxed the more alert became my mind.

When Idosa had completed telling us some things about the temple and the future I am not allowed to tell, he said that we should sit on each side of the triangle. The blue flame was left at the tip of the triangle. This placed Robert in one corner, myself in the second, and the flame in the third. I sat in the lotus posture, and Robert cross-legged. Idosa took his place in front of us. He lifted his arms and hands. He also lifted his eyes, and prayed again.

And then something happened. I swear I never saw Idosa place it there for his hands were stretched upward, but as I watched him I caught first just a glint of it in the blue light. Then, as I stared, it became more apparent, until I was gazing at a gleaming star on the breast of Idosa. It was hung about his neck from a chain. Now for those who doubt me, I will admit that he may have placed it there earlier during our conversation, and I failed to notice it until now. But since I am sworn to tell the truth in this account, I must swear that, so far as I am able to tell, the star simply materialized there before my eyes.

It was apparently crystal for it reflected the light of the blue flame, yet it seemed also to have some singular light of its own. At any rate, there it hung, sparkling and clear. The blue flame which was behind us seemed now to be in front of us, as its reflection was caught in the center of the crystal star.

Idosa finished his prayer, and lowered his hands. He made no explanation of the star, except to say, "Perhaps at some time in the future we can bring one to you at Astara, through apport means, and it shall be a constant reminder of this day in your lives, and for all Astarians to behold."

This promise filled us both with great hope that some time a crystal star may be brought to us during one of Robert's classes at Astara by one of the Masters, so that all may share with us its beauty and its reality. (Since this record was written, a magnificent crystal star has been apported to Astara during a class and has been set in an appropriate mounting. I wear it often during church services, when I teach seminars, and when I conduct Fire Initiation ceremonies. A picture of it is shown later.)

My mind was filled somewhat with disappointment. So far we had seen none of the things I had visioned. I had anticipated that several, if not many, of our Teachers would manifest for our ceremony ... perhaps some of those yet living in the physical body. I had hoped that the mystic ones who were purported to live at Shasta would appear. Yet here we were with no one present save Idosa. He seemed to read my thoughts, for he said, "There are many present, Little One, as you shall discover."

Then he raised his hands again. He asked us to fasten our eyes upon the flame in the star and to concentrate upon his chant. His voice began a slow chant, the words sounding something like this: *Om buhu ... Om buvaha ... Om swaha!* I memorized the sound of the words. However, since they are not English, I feel sure the spelling is incorrect.

I was unaware of time. I was keenly aware of the sensation I was experiencing within myself. Idosa's eyes no longer twinkled. They were like dark pools of night there above the blue flame. The top of my head seemed to be slowly expanding, as if a door were being gradually opened. My body was "melting" — simply dissolving — and I was floating up out of it. At no time did I experience a lapse of consciousness, only

a falling away of my physical body. My consciousness was expanding out through the top of my head.

The chant stopped, and Idosa stood there poised a moment, and then started another chant. I cannot tell you the words of it. I am not sure I even remember them correctly, even the sound of them, and if I did I could not tell you, for I am forbidden.

The words were magic ... that is the only way I can describe them. Soon after they were begun, the "door" in the top of my head slid completely back. My feet seemed to have vanished, my hands, and entire body ... none were any longer a part of me, for I had expanded out and out, until actually I seemed to encompass the universe itself. I have understood for a long time what John of Patmos meant when he said, *I was in the Spirit on the Lord's day, and heard behind me a great voice, as of a trumpet ...* and I have before now taken astral flights and remembered them, but this was incomparable to those other flights. I was indeed *in the Spirit.*

The star at which I gazed appeared to be coming nearer and nearer to me, and growing in size, until I suddenly rose right though the center of it, and I remembered no more.

When next I became aware of anything, I was blinking my eyes because of the brilliant light in which I was surrounded. It was as if I had been asleep and someone had turned on a bright light to which I could not adjust my eyes. Slowly, everything came into focus. I knew immediately that I had stepped out of my body, for I could see it in repose there on the slab. Robert stood beside me, as did Idosa. I looked toward the source of the blinding light. It came from the dome over us, which resembled transparent silver, if that term can be visualized. It glistened like silver in the sun, yet it seemed as if we could see right through it.

As my eyes slowly adjusted, I became aware of the walls about us. If the walls of colored stone in the earthly Cave had been beautiful, these quite took my breath. They seemed to be solid with jewels.

I do not mean the walls of this *Astral Temple* were laid in earthly jewels. What I am trying to say is that the flashing brilliance of these walls was superior to any earthly temple whose walls might have been laid with gems.

As I stared open-mouthed at the wonder of it, I realized something that helped me to understand many things I had heard of Shasta. Many tales had been told of magnificent temples there, and some writers declared they had seen them. It is quite clear that, in actuality, there are no earthly temples built there which the eyes could see, but there are incredibly beautiful astral temples there. It is without doubt true that they "saw" the temple they described, but with astral vision, as I was now seeing it. When Idosa had told us there were no temples visible to the eye, but only the retreats within the heart of the Mount, I had not suspected the presence of these temples of the astral built here, nor had he revealed the secret.

As my awareness stabilized in ever-expanded consciousness, I became aware for the first time of the apparel I was wearing. I wore a robe of the most exquisite gossamer "cobweb." It floated like a vaporous cloud about me. It was white ... and yet with every movement of my body its substance seemed more light than white, as reflections caught interwoven silvery threads. About my waist I wore a wide girdle of indescribable essence. The sandals on my feet consisted simply of soles, and ties wound about my feet and ankles.

I looked at Robert. He wore a cassock-styled tailored robe, similar to some I have seen members of the clergy wear here on the earth plane. It was also white, except that around the hem was a wide band of peculiar symbols and hieroglyphic figures embroidered in dull old gold. He wore no belt, for his robe was form-fitting. The neckline of his robe was cut high, giving the appearance of the "backward" collars worn by some clergy. I remembered past conversations with him when I suggested that perhaps he should wear clergy collars of this type, and his immediate and vehement rejection of the idea, and I almost laughed aloud.

I looked at Idosa. His robe was similar to Robert's. He asked us to follow him. He led the way toward a great door. As we approached it, I looked back to see our three physical bodies left there in the Mystic Cave. Idosa apparently, while still in his body, had sat down before us, and all three bodies were in a deep trance. I must pause here in my story for a moment to speak of something which I asked if I might tell you, and I have permission.

IF YOU ARE AN ESOTERIC SEEKER you probably will have read fragmentary sketches of initiation ceremonies in ancient days — of the postulant who is brought before the Hierophant; of the secret Word and Sign; of tests and trials to be faced; of the ordeal; of the ultimate initiation ... about which very little has ever been revealed. Perhaps much has been revealed in this report by what I have already written — more than is usually described. In this particular initiation, Robert and I were the candidates, the postulants. Idosa was the Hierophant. The Hierophant is the High Priest or Priestess, except that in *real* initiations he or she is much more than that. For instance, in Masonic initiations the Worshipful Master would be the equivalent of the Hierophant, except that today he possesses no unusual powers, he simply bears the title. The dictionary calls the Hierophant "the expositor of Sacred Mysteries." Thus the *true* Hierophant possesses powers of true mastership.

The candidate is placed in a trance by the Hierophant. Now there are those who will say that the candidate is simply hypnotized. This is not a fact. True hypnotism is indeed a marvelous thing, but it is only the incipient stage of the high art of inducing trance. The Hierophant — this great occult Magician — must not simply hypnotize the candidate ... but must be able to induce a trance and cause the soul-body to separate from the physical body without breaking the thread of consciousness on the astral plane. Observe the difference. Also observe the difference between this type of trance and the ordinary trance.

The Hierophant must not only induce this trance state within the candidate, but in him or herself as well. For as the candidate gains awareness on the astral plane, so do they find the Hierophant there to meet the candidate, to be guided through the real initiation which always occurs on the astral or perhaps even higher level. All the while, the Hierophant must keep intact the thread of consciousness within the candidate so that they will vividly remember the initiatory experience in the spiritual realms.

Thus you can see that the Hierophant is far more than a hypnotist. However, hypnotism is a step in the right direction, IF the "operator" is a student of mysticism and not a mere dabbler in a science which can be extremely dangerous unless understood and properly practiced.

I have given far more than a hint of one of the great secrets of initiation. Perhaps you already knew of it, perhaps not. I am sure I would not have been allowed to write of it unless the Masters wanted it revealed. You see, many are beginning to remember much that occurs to the soul while the physical form is sleeping, and many are experiencing initiation on the astral and remembering flashes of it. Therefore, the Teachers feel it wise to reveal this aspect of the procedure adopted during ceremonies in ancient days. However, this is only one small part of the total ceremony of initiation. There is much more about which I cannot now speak.

I have said that Idosa led us toward the door of another room. We entered, and were delighted to find there a host of friends

waiting our arrival. As we entered they rose from their seats and began singing a "welcome" song, much as we sing Happy Birthday here on the earth plane. (A similar happening occurred when, many years later, I entered the King's Chamber in the Great Pyramid in Egypt — I intuitively heard a chorus of angelic voices chanting a welcome.) When they finished the song, they raised their hands in the secret Sign of the ancient Order of Melchizedek, of which Astara is a branch. Then bedlam broke loose as all solemnity was dropped, and they rushed forward to greet us. There were so many dear ones, and many Workers from Astral Astara, many Astarians who had passed from Earth into higher life. There were Teachers and Masters of the Mysteries.

After a time of visiting together and experiencing the incredible sensation of bodily freedom, I noticed that one by one the visitors had stopped speaking and stood looking toward a great arch. I followed their gaze and saw outlined there the Egyptian Priest-King Zoser. It is Zoser who has charge of the Healing Shrine at Astral Astara, and he it is who performs such miraculous healings for many Astarians and friends of Astara on Earth. Robert and I instinctively started toward him.

Zoser, the Priest-King of ancient Egypt. He appeared to both Robert and me during the days when we were in retreat from the world in 1951 to receive instructions from our unseen Teachers as to how and where to establish Astara. It was then Zoser first stepped into our lives, promising to overshadow the healing ministry of Astara, and it is through the miracles of his healing efforts that Astara has become renowned as a center of healing.

Zoser, of Astara

Remembering that he had been an Egyptian King when he lived on Earth, I wondered how we should react, how we should greet him. Should we bow low? Should we kneel? I have seen him many times in visionary form during meditation — or when I have been projecting White Light healing to petitions sent from Astarians, but never had I beheld him so that I might touch him personally and speak directly to him.

He solved the problem by spreading wide his arms and we walked straight into them. He placed one about Robert and one about me, and drew us close as a father would his children. A moment later, he placed a hand on each of our heads and spoke his blessings over us. The touch of his hand was like a charge of high voltage electricity. The current swept from my head to my feet and rippled outward from me like an etheric tidal wave.

He led us then toward the center of the room and someone handed him a rolled scroll, which he began to unroll. Everyone except Robert and myself seemed to know what was coming next. Zoser read a name. That person walked toward the great carved arch leading out of the temple. He stopped as he reached the arch and stood with his back to us, at one side of the arch. Zoser called another name. Another walked toward the arch and took his place on the other side of it. As more names were called, they went forward and took their places.

Two lines were forming, with a wide space between them. They faced toward the arch. When every name had been called, and the two lines formed, Zoser placed Robert at the end of one line and me at the other. He took his place between us, and the two lines marched out of the temple.

As we neared the arch, I noticed a sentence written in a strange language over the curve of it ... probably Sanskrit. I made a note in my mind to ask someone what that sentence said, but in the events ahead I forgot it.

 AS WE STEPPED THROUGH the arch of the temple, we found the world without lighted but dimly, as if by moonlight, but I saw no moon. I recalled that it was still midday in the earth world, and very warm. I looked for the sun. I saw it not. Nor was the heat of the physical plane in effect. There was a delightful mellow glow over everything, and it was quite enchanting. Overhead floated white clouds. I saw something that, again, made me want to laugh hilariously — maybe even hysterically. Winding down the side of the verdant mountain was a smooth path! It led down, down the way we had come up. I remembered the difficult, the horrendous, climb we had in reaching the Cave. I did not laugh, because the path itself seemed to be a reminder that we had been forced to climb the mountain as a last trial of our desire for initiation. This smooth path, of course, was on the astral, and there was not one on the physical plane.

There was also another path leading up and up, and the leaders of our procession started toward it. It led up the side of Mount Shasta itself, and my eyes followed it all the way to the top. There I beheld a scene which defies description. There rose the most magnificent Cathedral I have ever beheld. Earth has no equal. The Astral Cathedral sat directly over the inner Great Temple at the peak of Mount Shasta, about which Idosa had spoken earlier. The Cathedral covered the entire peak of the Mount. The brilliance of it so dazzled me, I had to momentarily avert my eyes. It shone as if it were made of innumerable diamonds, all flashing in the midday sun, except there was no sun. The dome of the Temple rose high, high into the sky. And there, over the dome, rising yet higher into the sky, was a glorious glittering Star which revolved around and around, very slowly, as a beacon light does here on the earth plane.

The wonderment of it was quite overwhelming, and the procession paused to give both Robert and me an opportunity to leisurely survey this Cathedral of the Star. It was strange but, instead of rapture, I felt the tears pour down my face. I was remembering a recurring dream and vision I had seen of a Temple for Astara on the earth plane. Rising over it was a star such as the one I now beheld raying out its light over this incomparable Cathedral. As we watched, the star slowly revolved, projecting its beams of light far into the sky.

We journeyed on, and although from where we were to the top of Mount Shasta itself must have been several miles as measured by Earth distance, still we walked with the greatest of ease and covered the ground in very little time. The procession halted at the entrance to the Cathedral and each line stepped to one side and faced inward, so that as Zoser led us forward we marched between the two long lines, with all of them facing us, their hands lifted in the secret Sign. The great doors opened as we approached. We entered. The procession fell into step behind us.

I do not know if I can describe what we beheld inside that wondrous Temple. I have spent much time pondering just what words might help you visualize it; or something with which I might compare it that would help you to "see" it. But on Earth I have never seen such walls, nor such immensity. The nearest comparable description of the walls is to ask: are you familiar with crystal, white crystal? You know how there are splashes of color often found in crystal — especially that which has been exposed to the sun? Well, these walls seemed to be made of white crystal, with patches of every color imaginable interspersed — not vivid, but very muted and subdued. Some areas were highly polished and radiated a glow. Others were rough hewn, just as natural crystal stone is carved in marvelous patterns by nature. That does not sound necessarily beautiful at all, does it? Ah, but I wish you might

have seen it for yourself ... then you would know. If this meager
description of it can give you even a vague idea, I am happy.

Zoser led us on through the Temple and we approached a wall. It
was made of this same crystal, polished and shining — but embedded in it, as though nature had carved it, was a seven-pointed Star
with the All-Seeing Eye in its center. It was the same symbol Idosa
had worn on his wrist bracelets. Even as in his, the Great Eye here
seemed to be made of special crystal which reflected the colors of
all about it. We expected a door to open to let us pass. But it did
not. Instead, Zoser spoke a soft chant of special words and a center
panel of the entire wall softly slid upward. We passed through into
an enormous hall. Zoser stopped us at a certain point, and the procession divided and proceeded toward one end of the hall. Arriving
there, each one removed their shoes, then was seated. I have never
beheld a hall of such magnitude, and I doubt if there will ever be
a facsimile built on the earth plane. It was like a mammoth arena
— one built for extraordinary events. Our company occupied only
one small area of it.

Zoser and Robert and I had stepped upon a slightly raised dais
at one end of the hall. The procession was quickly seated, and everyone faced toward a certain wall. At first I failed to understand
why, but as quietness settled down over us the wall began to lift,
very slowly. When it was completely lifted, I understood what was
meant by the Temple Veil in ancient temples of worship. There it
hung before us in all its glory. It was tremendous in size. It, like
my robe, was of sheer gossamer cobwebs. It was no *one* color; it
was all colors blended together. It began to sway slightly back and
forth, as if moved by some mysterious force, and as it swayed and
the light skipped over it, the interblended colors were revealed. It
was like a stupendous iridescent floating flat soap-bubble ... first
blue, then silver, next a flash of crimson, and then flowing gold,
and on and on — the colors changing as it swayed in the lights.

The Veil began to part slowly, and when it finally was drawn back I knew we stood before the Holy of Holies. I understood why each member of our company had removed their shoes.

It is difficult to know just what to describe first. I suppose the altar should come first. There were seven steps leading up to it. On the first one stood a receptacle upon which sat another of the lamps from which burned another blue light. This lamp was much larger than the one we had seen before. At the top of the steps sat a chest, an enormous carved chest. It was too large to call a chest, but I have searched for a better word and found none. It was as large as a small house. It seemed to be made of old ivory trimmed with solid gold. Drapes covered the entire wall on either side of the altar, and had been drawn back to reveal the altar and chest.

In front of the altar, and between us and the altar, was a semi-circle of thirteen chairs. The chairs were turned toward the altar, with their backs to us. One of the chairs, huge and carved, resembling a throne, sat directly in front of the blue light, and facing it. There were six chairs on either side of it, forming the half-circle before the altar.

When the Veil had begun to part, the entire group had risen to its feet and begun a soft chant. Zoser now led us off to one side, preparing to take us toward the altar. As he stood there, waiting, as if for a cue, I suddenly became aware there were occupants in the chairs, as if they had slowly materialized. There sat twelve Master Teachers, among them our beloved Rama and Kuthumi. The large throne facing the blue light was empty — the thirteenth chair.

I noticed, as we stood waiting, and the chanting continued, that many people looked toward the ceiling often and I glanced upward. In the center of the great circular dome over us was a rotating circle of some strange magnifying glass. I nudged Robert. He looked up. We guessed that the Star outside which

rotated and sent beams of light into the sky might be attached to this revolving circle. Later on, we understood better the purpose of the magnifying glass. If the rotating Star outside was attached to it, it had no connection to what we witnessed later.

The masters Rama and Kuthumi rose from their chairs and walked toward the altar. They took their places on either side of the blue light, on the first step, and turned to face us and all the people gathered there. Zoser led us forward. My knees felt very weak, and for a fleeting moment, I gripped Robert's hand. Then Zoser placed Robert in front of Rama. He placed me before Kuthumi.

Rama, the Master Teacher who overshadows Robert. It was when Robert was twenty-five and struggling with his decision whether or not to give up a lucrative career in the world of advertising and become a minister, that Rama appeared to his young disciple. He spoke not a word but simply raised his hands in a gesture of love and blessing. The impact of the vision alone so powerfully affected Robert, he immediately set his life goals toward service to Rama and the Hierarchy of Great Ones.

Rama of Astara

We realized it was all a part of ritual and formalities for Zoser spoke our names and presented us to the two Masters; he also made an appeal that we be considered for another initiation in view of past good works. He outlined some of our work with which they, of course, were well acquainted, having taken an active part in most of it themselves. We guessed that a formal ritual was carried out for every candidate, even as here on Earth we perform a certain ritual in our initiations in Eastern Star, Masonic Order, and so on.

Then Zoser ceased his speaking and withdrew, stepping backward away from us, and leaving us there. It was then that the part of the ceremony which applied to us as individual candidates began. In previous writings of this initiation, I was not given permission to disclose what occurred next in the ceremony. Since then, the teachers have granted us permission, stipulating that certain sections which would violate greater secrets be withheld.

Kuthumi stepped from the platform and led Robert and myself back to the center of the room, upon the raised dais, where two huge carved seats had been placed for us. We were seated in them.

The Masters who had been seated in the semicircle before the altar took places covering a wide area around us. Their seats formed a square about us. The corners were left vacant. They began a low chant which sounded not unlike a mournful melody. A procession entered, carrying a large peculiar stone which was placed in the East corner. It was not a gem, but it radiated brilliant colors. The Masters changed their chant. Another procession carried a second stone to the South corner. A third procession carried a similar stone to the West corner, and a fourth to the North.

The room was darkened save for these four brilliant stones, flashing in the four corners of the square about us. The Master Rama explained that the stones represented the Lords of Karma, stationed in the four corners of the Earth: the East, South, West and North. The Masters Rama and Kuthumi continued to stand by the side of our chairs in the center of the dais.

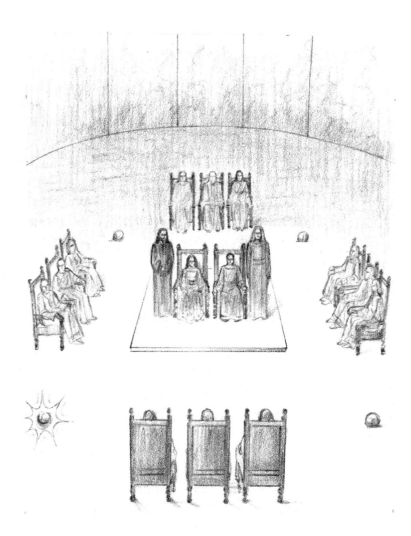

All the Masters faced the stone in the East and sang another chant. As the chant rose, so did the colors of the stone. Suddenly there was a blazing flash of light over it and the stone sank slowly into the floor, out of sight. The Master Rama explained to us that we were being presented to the Lords of Karma. (I cannot believe that actually the Lords of Karma were aware of us or this presentation. I believe it was simply a ritualistic part of the ceremony.)

We then faced the stone in the South; next, the stone in the West; and finally the stone in the North. Over each came the flash of light during the chant, followed by its disappearance into the floor, thus leaving the room in shadows. Dim lights burned somewhere, enough to cast a soft glow over the entire center of the enormous room.

One of the twelve Masters, whom we recognized as the Master Hilarion, announced that we were now to be presented with the "Triune Gifts" — representing the physical, mental and spiritual aspect of life. Another of the Teachers stepped forward and placed in each of our hands a staff upon which were represented all the herbs and fruits of Earth. The Master Zoser, who, when he lived upon the Earth, was deified by his people because of his healing powers, revealed to us much knowledge concerning the purity of the physical body and its importance in spiritual attainment.

He spoke much of healing and the Healing Staff which had just been presented to us. I cannot disclose all he revealed, yet I may say that through the years of our earthly life, we shall constantly use this knowledge in healing our Astarian members everywhere. And even though the Healing Staff which he presented to us is on the Astral, we shall many times draw upon it for healing power in restoring health to those in need.

The second staff presented to us was the "Wand of Hermes," or Caduceus, which represents the spinal column of the human being, the Tree of Life. In this initiatory drama, the Caduceus represented the mental aspect of life. It would require too long to enumerate the points of the discourse concerning the mastery of the mind in human evolution.

It appeared that to present to us the Gift representing the spiritual aspect involved more complications. For Robert and I were led away from the center of the room, to one side, and our two chairs were removed from the center of the dais. We saw a procession walk slowly toward the altar. They stopped at the mammoth Altar-Throne chair, the one directly facing the blue light and the altar — the one which had been empty. They lifted it and carried it back to the center of the dais, in the center of the room.

The Masters began another chant joined by other voices. One of the Masters stepped out of the square formation and walked slowly toward the magnificent Throne. He knelt before it. (I must omit some of the scene.) He ended his ritual by reaching out and lifting from the seat of the throne a cloth which he tied about his waist. It resembled a Masonic apron. In the center of this white apron glowed a sign of the zodiac. He stepped backward away from the Altar-Throne chair and resumed his place. When he removed his apron from the seat of the Throne, it caused a small amount of light to glow from the seat.

Another Teacher stepped forward to the Altar-Throne, knelt, proceeded through the same ritual which I am not allowed to relate, took from the Altar-Throne seat another apron which bore a different zodiacal sign, tied it about his waist, stepped backward and proceeded to his former place. The removal of his apron caused still greater light to emit from the seat.

As each Teacher took an apron, the light became more brilliant. Also it soon became apparent that the Teachers were forming a circle about the Throne, instead of resuming the square. When the last apron was removed from the Altar-Throne, the light from the seat was blinding. The Twelve Teachers faced the throne, each of them wearing a different sign of the zodiac upon the apron. I cannot tell you the ritual which followed, except to say that they were paying reverent homage to the Solar Deity, as represented by the Altar-Throne. As their chants rose, so did the light from the Throne until it seemed to me the light matched that of the sun.

The mantrum ended abruptly. Kuthumi and Rama stepped from their places in the circle toward the front of the throne. We were told to go to them. Again, I felt an inner weakness. I do not like to admit it, but truly I must say that I felt so completely awed it bordered on fear. I tried to walk but my legs would not move. The scene was frightening. "I'm going to faint ..." I whispered to Robert.

Kut-Hu-Mi, of Astara

Kuthumi (sometimes spelled Koothumi) is the Master who overshadows my writings and teachings, not only in this present life but in several previous lifetimes. He is the Source of my inspiration in the writings of Astara's Degree teachings, "The Book of Life," and "The Great Work of the Penetralia," the teachings of ancient wisdom in my books, Lessons, and seminars.

And then I saw my Master Teacher, Kuthumi, turn his face directly toward me. I looked at him. I am sure he sensed my inadequacy. His black eyes were focused squarely upon me. I want to say that it is near impossible to look the Master in the eye. The rays projecting from them are so powerful as to be almost paralyzing. It is like looking into the sun. But to the

extent that I was able to meet his eyes, I discerned the shadow of a smile. Ever so slightly, he lowered his head as if nodding to me. I felt Robert's hand on my back, urging me forward — and suddenly we were walking and walking and walking. We entered the circle formed by the Teachers, and continued until we reached the two Masters. They indicated we should face the Altar-Throne, and to step toward it with them.

As we approached it, the light from the Throne became brighter and brighter, until suddenly it burst into what appeared to be brilliant white fire. I had often wondered what I should do when the time arrived for me to face the Initiation by Fire. I thought, with no slight misgivings, that we were to be asked to walk directly into this white fire. But we paused immediately before the Throne and were told to kneel.

The two Masters stepped past us to either side of the Throne and turned to face us. From receptacles on either side of the Throne, they dipped their hands in Holy Oil and made the sign of the cross on our foreheads. Then they each reached into the receptacle again. Taking out objects which they first held high in the air, they placed them about our necks.

To Robert, Rama presented an amulet of the All-Seeing Eye. The Master Kuthumi presented a brilliant seven-pointed star to me, with a crystal glowing in its heart. I must attempt to describe what occurred as the amulets fell about our necks.

The white fire of the Throne mounted higher and higher, until just as the spiritual gifts were placed about our necks and fell into place, an actual explosion erupted from within the Throne, sending blazing sparks upward to shower down on us, covering us completely, and the two Masters. I was startled at first, but immediately realized there was no heat in the sparks. When you were a child, do you remember lighting sparklers on the Fourth of July? Do you remember that the sparks which blaze and fly in wild commotion possess no heat? It was the same with this miniature volcanic eruption of white spiritual fire.

I cannot describe the sensation I experienced in my consciousness during this baptism by Fire ... this Fire Initiation ... except to say that my soul was lifted into realms of spiritual ecstasy for which there are no human words ... for which there is no human understanding. Any attempt to soil this experience by attaching words of Earth to it would be sacrilegious. I should say that all during the ecstasy, I felt the dark eyes of Kuthumi piercing through the Fire, raying an incredible power into my Third Eye.

As the sparks of the Fire died down, so did the light of the Altar-Throne. The Teachers — all save Rama and Kuthumi — chanted a mantrum in unison, softly, as the light slowly faded. The two Masters made a final sign of the cross over us as the light went out.

Thus ended our Fire Initiation Ceremony. In the dimness which followed, the Throne was carried back to its place in the Holy of Holies, and the Masters retired therein also. The Temple Veil closed once again upon the altar. Then our many friends surrounded us, wishing us joy, congratulating us as we do friends here on Earth after realizing some momentous achievement. This was a time of supreme happiness for both of us. Our hearts were filled with that indescribable humble pride one experiences when, at the close of a day, you review your work and find it well done. Or, graduating from a training period, you receive recognition through the presentation of a higher degree.

Our festivities had continued for a while when we became aware that other activities were about to transpire. I cannot stress too strongly that what happened next had no connection whatever to us or to our initiation. The scene which followed our initiation and which we witnessed occurs frequently there in the temple, and the fact that it

took place at the time we were privileged to be there does not mean that it had anything to do with us. But we shall be eternally thankful that we were allowed to remain and witness it.

 IT DID NOT TAKE US LONG to notice that, in addition to our many friends who had come to witness our initiation ceremony, others who were complete strangers began arriving. They took seats much as one does when attending any church service, except that these seats formed an immense circular arena. There was an air of tense excitement, and finally we asked what was happening. Someone suggested we just wait and see for ourselves; that we were about to witness something that would change our very lives, and which we could relate to you.

As I have told you, the temple was enormous, but until now I had no idea just how immense it really was. People by the hundreds arrived, and wall after wall slid up, revealing more and more seats. No one would give us a hint of what was about to happen. So we took our seats with the rest of our friends and waited. A great sea of people soon completely filled the place. The outer doors of the temple were closed. The lights were lowered until it was quite dark. All was still and quiet. An undercurrent of tense excitement — of hushed anticipation — pervaded the atmosphere.

The wall in the Temple began to rise again — the one revealing the temple Veil. The Veil parted again — rippling in glorious colors — and the Masters sat in their chairs in a semicircle around the altar. The thirteenth chair, the Altar-Throne chair, was still vacant.

I had to strain to see what happened next for the light was dim. The lid of the great carved chest on the altar began to lift, and there began to unroll and rise out of it what appeared to be a bright silver screen, not unlike a movie screen. But it appeared far more brilliant, more like a mirror with a silver surface. So far as I could tell, it WAS a mirror. Then all was quiet for what seemed an interminable time. What could have been a restless crowed waited calmly and silently. I marveled at the quiet, tense patience.

I asked a friend what caused the delay. He said, "We are waiting for a certain star to move into a certain meridian in the heavens. When it does, the beams from it will shine down through that magnifying glass in the top of the dome up there above us, directly on that mirror before us, and then ... you shall see."

Robert asked, "Do you mean that the stars which we can see on the earth plane also can be seen here on the astral?" And the friend replied, "THIS one can." He offered no further explanation for a faint light had begun to appear on the "mirror" before us.

The light grew slowly brighter until, finally, the mirror was completely lighted. The entire room was dark save for a shaft of light pouring down through that circle of magnifying glass in the dome. As we watched, a cloud appeared on the mirror. It began to take shape. It became clearer and deeper until we beheld a form taking shape. As the form gradually condensed, I thought — could it be *He*? — Could it truly be *He*? And then the shadowy form suddenly came into clear focus — and there stood the beloved Master Jesus radiantly and majestically before us. For a moment I stopped breathing — in fact, my total being was suddenly held in suspension, so startled, so awed was I. Could this be possible? Were we indeed worthy to be present at such an august gathering? What had he come to say? Were we to be fortunate enough actually to see and hear words and teachings from the One we so long had served?

It would be a grave mistake to indicate that the Master himself stood there, for He did not. However, he did stand, at that moment, somewhere on some higher plane and spoke the words

which he spoke to us. We *were* privileged to hear his words and see the reflection of his image, much as we view television in our homes today. Do not ask me how. I think the process we now call holography might explain it. I only know it was through some cosmic "hookup" on the spirit planes of life. We were told that many other groups were gathered together in other temples throughout many planes of life to hear Him. Thus millions — perhaps billions heard his voice and saw his regal form. This I did learn ... and that He spoke often by this means, teaching and guiding people.

He began to speak. His words flowed from the entire "mirror," it seemed, and not just from his lips. The voice itself was like a wondrous melody. He spoke of many things which would take too long to tell, nor would I be allowed to share some of them. Although His coming was not connected in the slightest with our initiation, still he seemed to be aware that we were present, because — ever so fleetingly — He once focused his splendid eyes directly upon us, as He spoke of grave conditions existing on Earth today.

He spoke of the chaos and the turmoil. He said that the planet Earth was leaving behind a certain field of expression — the Piscean — and entering a new one — Aquarius. The new field of Aquarius would gradually increase in rarified ethers, and many types of souls expressing on the planet today would not be able to withstand these higher vibrations. Therefore when they met their physical death, their souls would be left behind in the old Piscean field of etheric and vibrational expression to wait the coming of another planet entering that field. On that Piscean planet they could again take up bodies of flesh and continue their evolution in ethers compatible with their degree of inner light.

The earth planet would move slowly out into the Sixth Dispensation. Souls in the realms of spirit who were abiding in the Aquarian field of expression into which the planet was moving would be waiting to take upon themselves bodies of flesh and express once again on Earth. One by one they would incarnate again. However, since they were more highly evolved than those left behind in the old Piscean field, little by little the chaos would die away. Little by little inspired and advanced souls would come forth as leaders. Little by little nations would learn to live together in peace; little by little, the law of love would begin to manifest, and human beings would begin to realize that they cannot hurt their brother or sister without likewise hurting themselves ... and although this is a selfish way to love, nevertheless, it is a beginning.

He said the planet as a whole has created for itself much adverse karma, and that this cosmic debt has to be discharged before the planet can enter fully into its new field of expression. Therefore, there must be what human beings call "destruction," but what the Masters call "change." There is, He indicated, no such thing as "destruction," only transformation, a passing away of the "old" and a coming forth of the "new."

He spoke of ever-increasing currents of magnetism over the western part of North America. He did not say so in exact words, but we assumed he meant that we should not flee to some other part of the nation in the hope of escaping earthquakes or floods. He said that there are methods we know not of to protect those who are Light Workers.

He said that prayer and devotion to good works built about the soul an "armor of light" against which no evil can prevail. He reminded us that although "ten thousand might fall by your side, it shall not come nigh thee — for we shall give our angels charge over the children of light."

He said He had come when the planet was entering the Piscean Age two thousand years ago. The planet was immersed

in the clouds of darkness created by the mass consciousness of the human race — the condensed thought forces of hatred, wars, greed, jealousies, lust, violence. To make it possible for the lifewave of souls to pass with the planet into the field of Pisces, He had taken upon Himself the dark karma of the entire human race. Other Master Teachers representing other spiritual traditions had done the same, at different times, to send Light to the lifewave of humanity. This sacrifice had purified the ethers of Earth, giving the evolving souls a new beginning. Thus He had "died for our sins," our karma, so that we might have a new opportunity to apply the laws of love He brought, taught and demonstrated.

Now, He said, the planet approaches once again a "new birth." And once again it is immersed in the shadow-thoughts of hate, war, greed — and fear. The clouds of karma are heavy and dark about us. But, He said, there also radiate forces of light — much more than was evident when Earth entered Pisces two thousand years ago.

Rising among the karmic clouds of darkness are the streams of light force, dispelling the darkness. Although the planet has created the possibility for destruction, it has also created the potential for salvation. Thus, He said, humanity faces a struggle. Each person, no matter how spiritually evolved must still give strength to the light within him or herself, rather than to the darkness, for we each have a mixture of both. Both aspects of self are to be accepted and to be loved, ever increasing the light force and power within.

Also, light workers must not give way to fear and predictions of chaos. Sending White Light, healing and love to everyone, all forms of life, to the planet Earth and to life everywhere, and asking for healing forgiveness for past errors will bring about positive transformation and will erase negative karma. Falling too much under the spell of fear, getting too caught up in the predictions of disaster, will be the mistake. For this only creates more fear, and can render people immobile rather than actively working for positive change.

But, He said, enough light is now being disseminated to warrant aid from cosmic forces. Destruction of the planet will not be allowed, He promised. But it will require, he warned, supreme effort on the part of those who disperse the light. Their efforts must be untiring. They must not only enter the light themselves, but must show others the way — rather *THE WAY,* by example, not by preaching or attempting to control.

In the end, He promised, "the light from the prayers, the petitions, the service, the sacrifices of the children of light will enable the Cosmic forces to bring the planet and the "saved" of humanity into a "new heaven and a new Earth." He was not speaking of "saved" lives. He was speaking of the souls "saved" for this lifewave — those who would pass with the planet into a new and better Age, a new and better etheric atmosphere, a new and better spiritual radius.

You must interpret this part of His words as you so choose. There will evidently be difficulty — there will also be opportunity for spiritual growth, and for the transition into greater light for our planet and every form of life on it.

Then He dropped the subject of "destruction" and spoke of the wonders waiting ahead for the souls of Earth's lifewave. He spoke of many coming "discoveries" which would be part of the coming new age. He spoke of the birth of highly advanced Teachers. He spoke of the coming of Temples of Learning in which these Teachers would teach, so that people might learn more of cosmic laws and how to use them.

He spoke of the return of the "space people," bringing to Earth once again their advanced knowledge. Some would come from distant planets and others from etheric realms.

Ah, indeed, there is a Great Day coming. Let us learn to think not in terms of "destruction," but of light force and love force. And become aware that no matter what comes, on whatever plane of life you find yourself, you will continue to do the very best you can for GOOD. With such thoughts flowing among us, we can counteract the dark karma and much of the destruction can be avoided. To the degree that we do good, to the degree that we disseminate light and love, to that same degree will the clouds of karma be dispelled and never come upon us. This I know, for He spoke of it.

His message to us was a long one, but no one seemed aware of it. All were poised eagerly to absorb every word. When He neared the end of His message and lifted his hands to bestow His grace, many fell to their knees. Some heads were bowed low; some lifted their faces and their hands toward Him. There were many different reactions, but all were expressions of love and humility. The voice ceased, He held his hands still toward us. The light began to fade until the form slowly disappeared from the mirror. The mirror sank slowly back into the great carved chest. The shaft of light coming down through the dome began to fade and the lights of the Temple began dimly to glow. No one moved. No one spoke — all reluctant to break the spell of His presence. For a long time, all these thousands of people sat, pensive and prayerful, experiencing true meditation together, absorbing into their minds all the words He had spoken. Then slowly and quietly some of them began to rise and slip away.

It was as we sat thus that I again felt my consciousness fading — like a sleep-trance stealing over me. I knew that Robert felt it, too. He reached out and took my hand. We did not need to speak to realize the time had arrived for us to be brought back to physical plane awareness. The dharma-duties of Earth waited, and the call to service resounded like the throb of a distant drum.

When I next opened my eyes, I was sitting again in my physical form in the Cave of the Mystic Circle. Robert was also stirring. Idosa was gone. I wondered where. Back to a somewhere city? — Or back to a somewhere space ship? — Or was he an angel in disguise?

A wise sage once said that God hides the glories of other realms of life so that human beings might endure life on the physical plane ... and it is true. What a prison is the physical body! The glories of the higher life are shown only to those who can view them, and who can turn again and take up earth life without vain dreamings of the life-to-be.

And so we came down from the mountain top a great deal changed from when we went up. We came down and returned to our beloved Astara and the Great Work — the Work we were sent to fulfill before we ever put on these forms of flesh.

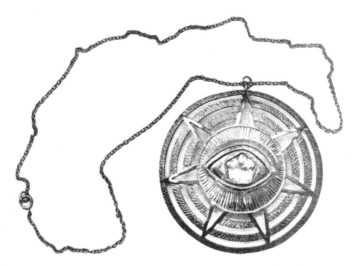

With what seems a fitting finale to my story, I share with you a picture of the amulet I often wear when I teach and heal at seminars all over the country. As was promised, the center crystal — a five pointed star — was apported to us. We had it mounted in a golden symbol embodying the All-Seeing Eye and Seven-Pointed Star. The crystal center came from the Great Ones whom we serve and radiates a remarkable power. The amulet was created as closely as possible to combine those our two Masters placed about our necks and over our hearts during the high point of our initiation.

If there are times when we seem restless among you, know that it may be because our souls are sometimes homesick for the soul realms of life. Know, too, that because of you, beloved seekers of the Light, our lives here on Earth have been unusually happy and blessed. The privilege of walking among you and serving you has made our lives worthwhile. May the blessings of the Masters abide with you until we meet together in the Land of the Blessed.

Selah

WHEN WE ASCEND
(Earlyne and Robert)

And it shall come to pass
That we shall walk the earthly ways no more —
We shall lay down the forms you touched
And dwell in fairer forms in lands beyond
    the mists —
Lest you should think we shall forget
That once we knew the darkness you
    sometimes know,
Remember this — it is not so.
Though lighter than the thistledown,
We shall be more enduring than the stars —
And when the shadows come we'll not be far
From the fingertips of your mind
Whispering a dream of love.
In moments when the stillness falls,
Listen for the mists to part —
We shall be melting in the moondrops of your
    meditations
While we write our names on the leaves of your
    heart.
We shall slip into your heartaches like a sigh slips
    into the ethers of dissolving smoke rings —
We shall be shadow-sharing all your joys and fears
    and castle-dreaming.
The seasons come, the seasons go,
But we shall constant be and true,
Because, beloved child of light,
We loved you better than you knew.

The publisher of this book is a nonprofit
organization presenting metaphysical,
mystical, philosophical and self-help
material. For more information go to:
astara.org

Made in the USA
Coppell, TX
19 June 2020